The
Carl Vinson Memorial
Lecture Series

INAUGURAL LECTURE

The
Carl Vinson Memorial
Lecture Series

INAUGURAL LECTURE

Negotiation:
The Alternative
to Hostility

PRESIDENT JIMMY CARTER

MERCER

MUP

Negotiation: The Alternative to Hostility
Copyright © 1984 by
Mercer University Press, Macon GA 31207
All rights reserved
Printed in the United States of America

Paperback edition 2003

Library of Congress Cataloging in Publication Data
Carter, Jimmy, 1924-
Negotiation, the alternative to hostility.

(The Carl Vinson memorial lecture series)
"Inaugural lecture."
1. Diplomatic negotiations in international disputes—Addresses,
essays, lectures. 2. Negotiation—Addresses, essays,
lectures. I. Title. II. Series.
JX4473.C37 1984   327.2   84-10720

ISBN 0-86554-882-X

Contents

The
Carl Vinson
Memorial Lecture Series

❧ INAUGURAL LECTURE ❧

Thursday
The Twenty-Eighth of April
Nineteen Hundred Eighty-Three

Eight O'Clock
Macon City Auditorium
Macon, Georgia

*The Carl Vinson Memorial Lecture Series
is made possible through the generosity
of John Adams Sibley*

The Carl Vinson Memorial Lecture Series

PROGRAM

Raleigh Kirby Godsey,
President of the University, Presiding

INVOCATION
William Augustus Bootle
Law School Alumnus and Senior United States
District Judge, Retired

TRIBUTE TO JOHN ADAMS SIBLEY
Robert Lee Steed
Law School Alumnus and Partner,
King and Spalding Law Firm of Atlanta

TRIBUTE TO CARL VINSON
Karl Patterson Warden
Dean, Walter F. George School of Law

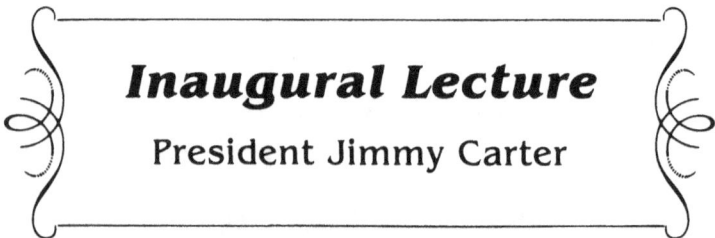

Inaugural Lecture
President Jimmy Carter

PRESENTATION
Lamar Rich Plunkett
Chairman, Mercer University Board of Trustees

The Carl Vinson Memorial Lecture Series Committee

James C. Rehberg, *Chairman*

John O. Cole
Ruth West Garrett
Sylvia G. Haywood
Harold S. Lewis, Jr.
Watson E. Mills
Karl P. Warden

ARRANGEMENTS AND PUBLICATIONS

University Office of Development
Emily P. Myers
Gloria O. McDaniel

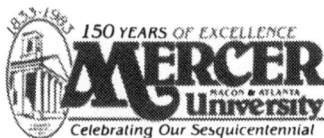

150 YEARS OF EXCELLENCE
MERCER
MACON & ATLANTA
University
Celebrating Our Sesquicentennial

Introduction

Remarks by

R. Kirby Godsey

President,
Mercer University

    It is a distinct pleasure to welcome you to the inaugural lecture of the Carl Vinson Memorial Lecture Series. This series has been made possible through the generosity of John Adams Sibley and it honors a great statesman of our time, Congressman Carl Vinson.

    This lecture is a major event in the celebration of Mercer University's Sesquicentennial Year—a year in which both the heritage and the promise of the university are brought into clear and dramatic focus. The sharing of these lectures with the public expresses the university's sense of continuity with this community, of which it is a part. The invitation to the public is a way of affirming this year that we see the progress and future of Mercer University to be closely linked with the community in which we serve.

COMMUNITY EVENT

The primary relationship of the university and the community is not institutional. Rather, the worth and the character of any community resides in the wisdom, the reason, the respect that are present among its people. The university and the people of Macon and Georgia share common hopes and dreams; and it is by our common devotion to the good, to the beautiful, and to the achievement of excellence in business, in learning, and in culture that we will build a community worthy of tomorrow's promise. We dedicate Mercer's Sesquicentennial Year to that end.

COMMON DEVOTION

Each of you honors us this evening with your presence. You have joined with us in a historic and memorable occasion. We are happy that you are here.

WELCOME

Judge William A. Bootle, senior judge in the United States District Court of Middle Georgia, and an alumnus of both Mercer University's Walter F. George School of Law and the College of Liberal Arts, will bring our invocation.

JUDGE BOOTLE

Robert L. Steed, a partner in the law firm of King & Spalding in Atlanta, and an alumnus of both the College of Liberal Arts and the Mercer Law School, and chairman of the Executive

ROBERT STEED

Committee of the Board of Trustees, will give a tribute to John Adams Sibley.

Karl P. Warden, dean of the Walter F. George School of Law, will tell us about the founding of the Carl Vinson Lecture Series and offer a tribute to the late Carl Vinson.

DEAN
WARDEN

No greater honor and no more distinguished beginning of the lecture series could come to Mercer University than to inaugurate the Carl Vinson Memorial Lectures in this manner on this evening. President Jimmy Carter honors Mercer University and Macon, Georgia, by his presence here this evening as the inaugural lecturer for the Carl Vinson Memorial Lecture Series.

PRESIDENT
CARTER

A Tribute
to John A. Sibley

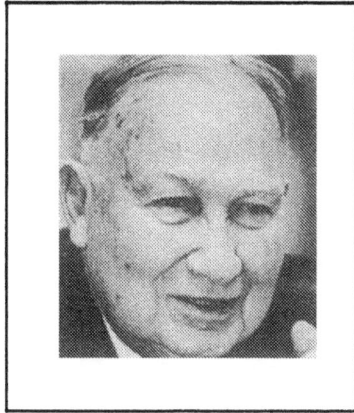

John Adams Sibley

For his leadership role as chairman of the education commission that in 1960 recommended retaining the public school system at all costs, John Adams Sibley is generally known as the man who saved public education in Georgia.

John Sibley earned the LL.B. degree from the University of Georgia in 1911, and practiced law in Milledgeville before joining the law firm of King and Spalding in Atlanta. He attracted national attention in the now-historic case of the *Coca-Cola Company v. Coca-Cola Bottling Companies*. Later he became general counsel to the Coca-Cola Company. He is a nationally recognized authority on corporate law.

Mr. Sibley is honorary chairman of the board of the Trust Company of Georgia and a director of the Coca-Cola Company. A charter and life trustee of the Walter F. George Foundation since 1947, Mr. Sibley has worked diligently on behalf of Mercer University's Walter F. George School of Law. His generous gift has made possible the Carl Vinson Memorial Lecture Series.

Address by

Robert L. Steed

*Chairman, Executive Committee,
Board of Trustees, Mercer University*

John Adams Sibley is a great American. To
enumerate the honors, directorships, professional, and business accomplishments of John
Sibley over his ninety-five years would take far
too much time on this occasion and would cause
him, I assure you, to grumble at me. With that
unhappy prospect firmly in mind, I will limit

this tribute to a few highlights of an incredibly
long and distinguished career as a lawyer, banker,
farmer, and statesman.

John Sibley is a native of Milledgeville and
obtained his law degree from the University of
DISTINGUISHED Georgia in 1911. He practiced law there for seven
CAREER years and was judge of the Baldwin County Court
from 1914 to 1918. In 1918 he came to Atlanta and
joined King & Spalding. In the 1920s he attracted
national attention as attorney for the Coca-Cola
Bottling Companies in a historic dispute with the
Coca-Cola Company and, as a result of his judi-
cious and successful settlement negotiations, he
secured the Coca-Cola Company as a client for
his firm. Later, on a leave of absence from his
firm, he joined the Coca-Cola Company as its
first general counsel and organized the law department of that company. He returned to King
& Spalding in 1940, but in 1946, at the request of
its client, Trust Company of Georgia, he with-
drew from the firm to become chairman of the
board and president of Trust Company of Georgia. He is now honorary chairman of the Trust
Company of Georgia and, I am happy to report
to you, keeps regular office hours in his seventh-
floor offices at Five Points.

As all of you know, he has long been a champion of education and is credited with saving
CHAMPION public education in Georgia. In 1960, at the age
OF of seventy-two, he took on the gruelling task of
EDUCATION heading what has come to be known as the "Sibley School Commission," which traveled about
the state holding hearings to gauge the true feel-
ings of Georgians on the then highly controversial question of integrating our public schools.

The hearings were televised and closely watched—in Georgia and throughout the nation. Mr. Sibley conducted them with fairness and gracious good humor. The result of this labor was a recommendation that the public schools of the state of Georgia be kept open.

His interest in agriculture and forestry is well known and dear to his heart. He has been described as keeping in intimate touch with the business end of the plow while molding his successful career as a lawyer and banker. LOVE OF THE LAND

He has served as chairman of the Board of Trustees for the Berry Schools in Rome and as chairman of the Board of Trustees of the Henrietta Egleston Hospital for Children in Atlanta. He holds honorary degrees from Oglethorpe, Emory, Morris Brown, Berry, and Mercer University. EDUCATION STATESMAN

Through his long personal friendship with Robert and George Woodruff, he has had a hand in directing hundreds of millions of dollars in gifts and grants from charitable foundations created by the Coca-Cola Company and on which he was a valued member. PHILANTHROPY

His interest in and generosity to Mercer has been long, legendary, and highly tangible. When the Walter F. George Foundation—our Law School's separate endowment—was organized in 1947, it was through the good efforts of John Sibley; he became a charter and life member of its Board of Trustees. WALTER F. GEORGE FOUNDATION

When I began the practice of law in 1962 I found, by happy circumstance, that my office was next door to that of John Sibley, and I was always pleased to find that he was so generous and A UNIQUE OPPORTUNITY giving of his time and attention. Of course, we were both just young men then—I was twenty-five and he was seventy-five. Seventeen years later, when we were presented with the possibility of acquiring the Insurance Company of North America building which now houses the Law School, I called on John Sibley to discuss what I thought to be a unique opportunity for us.

As chairman of the George Foundation, he suggested to Dr. Rufus Harris that we investigate the opportunity and undertake it if it appeared to be within our reach. As you may know, the money necessary to acquire the Law School campus and the INA building came from the Emily and Ernest Woodruff Fund—on which John Sibley and his longtime friend and fellow Walter F. George Trustee, George W. Woodruff, were active members. Through the good efforts of Mr. Sibley, the same sources made available the funds to acquire the Stratford Academy property next to the Law School, thus doubling the size of our campus and preserving a beautiful and significant piece of Macon's history—the Overlook Mansion.

On Saturday, 7 May, that mansion—now beautifully restored—will be dedicated as the Woodruff House, home of the John Adams Sibley Institute for Public Affairs. The activities of the institute will reflect the values associated with Mr. Sibley's life and service through research, lectures, workshops, conferences, seminars, and publications. President Kirby Godsey announced to the Trustees at our meeting on 15 April that the Sibley Institute would house the internationally prestigious Center for Constitu-

LAW SCHOOL BENEFACTOR

SIBLEY INSTITUTE

tional Studies, which will relocate from Notre Dame to Mercer University next year.

The Carl Vinson Memorial Lecture Series, conceived, created, and personally endowed by John Sibley, is inaugurated tonight to honor the memory of John Sibley's great friend and Mercer's great alumnus, the late Congressman Carl Vinson. For this particular constructive and generous act, for his prodigious friendship to Mercer throughout the years and for a life of extraordinary worth and service, I ask you all to join me in expressing our gratitude to John A. Sibley.

VINSON
LECTURES
FOUNDER

A Tribute
to Carl Vinson

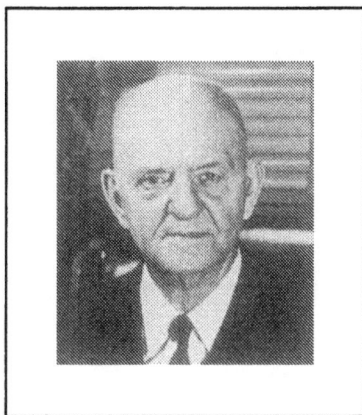

Carl Vinson

A 1902 graduate of Mercer University Law School, Carl Vinson practiced law in Milledgeville, and served as Baldwin County Prosecutor and as a state legislator. Beginning in 1914, he served twenty-six terms in the United States House of Representatives where he chaired the Armed Services Committee. He died in 1981 at the age of ninety-seven.

His election on 3 November 1914 to an unexpired term in the United States House of Representatives was followed by election to twenty-six consecutive terms in office. When he retired in January 1965, he had served a total of fifty years and one month in the House, a record that is still unsurpassed.

Mr. Vinson became the first living American to have a major naval warship christened in his honor with the launching in 1980 of the nuclear-powered aircraft carrier, the USS *Carl Vinson*.

The career of the late Carl Vinson was one of unparalleled service to his state and country.

Address by

Karl P. Warden

Dean,
Walter F. George School of Law

Welcome to the inaugural lecture in the Carl
Vinson Lecture Series of the Carl Vinson Public
Affairs Lecture Fund.

This lecture series has been conceived and
established by Mr. John Adams Sibley, a longtime trustee and chairman of the Board of Trustees of the Walter F. George Foundation. Mr.

Sibley and Congressman Vinson were lifelong friends.

The purpose of this lecture series is to honor Congressman Vinson by providing lectures of the very highest quality on legal and law-related subjects for the students and faculty of the Walter F. George School of Law, for other university students, faculty, and personnel, for alumni and friends of the School of Law and Mercer University throughout the world.

LECTURE
SERIES'
PURPOSE

Carl Vinson was born in Baldwin County, near Milledgeville, Georgia, on 18 November 1883. He graduated from Mercer University Law School in 1902. He practiced law in Milledgeville, worked as county solicitor, served in the Georgia House of Representatives and served as judge of the county court in Baldwin County. He was elected to the Sixty-Third Congress to fill an unexpired term on 3 November 1914. Woodrow Wilson was in the White House. The Springfield rifle was a major weapon in our defense arsenal. The winds of war were blowing in Europe.

VINSON
CAREER

In his first speech in Congress, the young freshman representative from Georgia said these words: "I devoutly hope that the casting of every gun and the building of every ship will be done with a prayer for the peace of America. I have at heart no sectional nor political interest but only the Republic's safety."

FIRST
SPEECH

Carl Vinson was the first person in the history of our nation to serve fifty years in the United States House of Representatives. He served with nine presidents. More than any other individual, Carl Vinson influenced and guided this nation through two world wars.

50 YEARS
IN THE
HOUSE

Many of you here this evening were present when in November 1973 Carl Vinson celebrated his ninetieth birthday with Mercer University Law School as this school celebrated its hundredth anniversary. This lecture series at Mercer's Law School honors one of our very own, one of our most distinguished alumni of all times—the late Carl Vinson.

MOST DISTINGUISHED ALUMNUS

Negotiation:
The Alternative
to Hostility

Address by

President Jimmy Carter

Carl Vinson Memorial Lecture
Mercer University
28 April 1983

About ten years ago I was here with the president of the United States to celebrate the Law School's one-hundredth birthday and Carl Vinson's ninetieth birthday. This year we would have celebrated Carl Vinson's one-hundredth birthday. Monday night I had supper with John Sibley, who is now ninety-five and, as you know, still going strong.

As I prepared this lecture, I felt honored, of course, at having been invited to deliver it, but also sobered and humbled to be part of a lecture series dedicated to a man like Mr. Vinson and

sponsored by a man like John Sibley. Both were dedicated to improving education, to maintaining the strength of our nation, to contributing to the search for peace, and to constantly striving for a higher standard of justice. They represented, in my judgment, the finest that Georgia and America have to offer.

Tonight I am going to speak about two words that I think epitomize their lives—justice

and peace.

This past weekend I spent several hours discussing with some of Georgia's most distin-

guished lawyers a question that is becoming ever more serious. How can we reduce the growing burden of unnecessary litigation that is overloading the system of justice in our country? In spite of some potential loss of legal fees if disputes are settled out of court, these attorneys all agreed that for their profession, for the court system, for our country, and for their clients, something had to be done. As you may have already guessed, we had a lot of discussion and did not come to any decisions or conclusions about exactly *what* should be done. When I got back to Plains, I picked up the phone and called my friend, Chief Justice Warren Burger. We had further discussion about this subject, one which, I have to tell you, we pursued on several occasions while I served in the White House.

The issue is very controversial, and I will relieve your minds by telling you this will not be the major topic of my talk. But it is one which is of great interest to everyone in the room, lawyer or not. I have found that a fresh approach is necessary if we are ever to move past such a persistent problem.

NEW
APPROACH
NECESSARY

To illustrate this point, I would like to tell you about a serious dispute between a student and his science professor. The student had received a zero on an exam question, and he insisted that he deserved a hundred. The question was: How do you determine the height of a tall building by using a barometer? The dean of the school was called on to referee the argument.

GROUNDS
FOR
DISPUTE

The science teacher insisted that the only proper procedure was that one should take a barometric reading at ground level, then carry the barometer to the top floor, take a different reading, and compute the height by the change in barometric pressure as is done with altimeters in an airplane. The student responded, "Using strictly scientific methods, I can determine the height of a building using a barometer in several different ways." The dean said, "If you can name three ways to determine the height of a building using a barometer, we'll give you a hundred." The student said, "That's fair enough."

ONLY
ONE
SOLUTION?

"First of all," he began, "you can take the barometer, put it on the ground, measure its height, and measure the length of its shadow. Then by measuring the length of the building's shadow, with simple arithmetic you can determine the height of the building. The second way," he continued, "is to take the barometer and a stop watch to the top of the building, release the barometer and time how long it takes to hit the

CREATIVE,
ALTERNATIVE
METHODS

ground. Again with simple arithmetic, strictly scientific, you understand, you can compute the height of the building. The third way," he finished, "is to take the barometer, tie a string on it, go to the top of the building, lower the barometer to the ground, and measure the length of the string."

The science professor was quite irate and claimed that he had been cheated. He refused to give the student a perfect grade. They decided to seek the advice of the provost of the university, who happened to be a professor in the business school. The student said, "Well, professor, if I had been asked the same question in a business class, I would have answered it this way: I would take the barometer to the basement of the building, walk to the engineer's office, and say, 'I have a nice barometer here, and I will give it to you if you will tell me how tall the building is.' " Well, the student won the argument and he got his perfect grade.

The point I want to make is this. We need the same kind of bright thinking, unanticipated approaches, and unorthodox ideas to achieve the ancient goals of better justice and peace in the world. Excessive litigation in our courts causes the backlog of cases to grow and the reputation of our system of justice to suffer. Some of these lawsuits go on ten or eleven or twelve years, as I observed with consternation while I was governor and president. Victory is more likely, as you can well imagine, for the litigant who can afford extended and very costly legal help. Even the fortunate party who eventually wins often has a hollow victory because of the time, bitterness,

and costs involved. There is a close parallel between a victor in litigation of this kind and a victor in a costly and bloody war.

Because of these problems lawyers and ju-
rists recently have begun to probe ever more ea-
gerly for alternative ways to resolve disputes,
away from impaneled juries and outside the
courtroom. Even trial lawyers who specialize in
this kind of litigation now realize that in many
cases their clients can best be served by settling
disagreements through mediation, negotiation,
or arbitration, or by agreeing to face-to-face discussions between the contending parties. Simply
going over the facts with unbiased and trusted
people can sometimes reveal that a relatively easy
settlement is possible.

TALKING
IT
OUT

Chief Justice Burger reported that a few
courses in dispute resolution have been initiated
in the finer law schools of our country and some
progress has been made in resolving actual cases
outside the courtroom. The three neighborhood
justice centers that I established as president,
with the help of Attorney General Griffin Bell, to
handle small claims and minor disputes, have
now increased to more than 200 throughout the
nation, and they are performing very well. There
has been a shift by some large corporations away
from regular litigation to the so-called mini-trial,
wherein the lawyers arrange for the principals to
meet personally to seek agreement. The most recent successful experience, Judge Griffin Bell
told me this weekend, was the *Borden v. Texaco*
case, which was resolved outside the courtroom
and involved claims of more than one billion
dollars.

LITIGATION
ALTERNATIVE

Carl Vinson Memorial Lecture

In spite of this progress, the chief justice concluded that, at best, we are holding our own and probably, he said, losing ground. He commented that in his earlier days the measure of a good lawyer was to represent his clients well and to keep them out of court. He deplored the growing tendency of many lawyers nowadays to assume that litigation is a natural and desirable process. He added that practicing attorneys are more concerned about the problem and trying harder to correct it than are the law schools in our country. Both of us agreed that more determined efforts and innovative ideas are necessary. The legal profession must not look on reform with excessive timidity. Justice can be delivered more efficiently and fairly. I have strong opinions concerning the need to provide relief for a seriously overloaded court system. There is, however, already a large volume of very fine literature on the subject, and the chief justice, Judge Bell, and many others are now speaking eloquently and with personal knowledge about it. Therefore, it is not my purpose tonight to enumerate options or recommendations concerning this problem.

Instead, I will concentrate on another aspect of my broader topic—one in which I have had some experience as president of the United States: the use of negotiation to settle differences between nations. Perhaps some of my own theories and practical knowledge can provide insights applicable to the resolution of other kinds of disputes—without litigation or war.

AN "UNNATURAL PROCESS"

THE NEGOTIATION ALTERNATIVE

When, in preparing for this lecture, I began to list the negotiations in which I had been personally involved, the number and diversity of them were quite a surprise. Also, I found that dispute resolution negotiations have become much more prevalent than a few decades ago—perhaps because of the threat of nuclear war, the reduction in oppressive colonialism, more rapid communications, and the proliferation of new nations and international organizations. There is a lot of literature on the subject, but most of it was not much help to me as president. Only the history of previous negotiations gave me much insight that I could use in the cases with which I had to deal.

INCREASING NEED

My primary and most important effort as president was to reduce to a minimum serious disputes, and to solve those most pressing ones which my predecessors left me. I will not take the time to discuss negotiations with NATO allies, South Africa, the Philippines, Greece, Turkey, and many others with whom we had difficult issues to settle. Instead, I have chosen just a few of the most highly publicized examples, and will use them to illustrate general procedures and principles which might be helpful in resolving other disputes. As you will soon remember, some of our efforts were disappointing, and an examination of the failures may also be informative. In some cases I was the personal negotiator, in others I monitored each step as performed by designated representatives, and at times my role was to prescribe a general formula or framework within which our negotiators or intermediaries had substantial latitude.

ILLUSTRATING PRINCIPLES AND PROCEDURES

The Panama Canal treaty negotiations were begun by President Lyndon Johnson, continued by President Nixon and President Ford, and finally concluded by me in two phases: First, with Panama during my first year in office; and second, several months later, with the individual members of the United States Senate, two-thirds of whom had to ratify the beneficial but very unpopular treaties before they could become effective. This was perhaps the most courageous act in the history of the United States Senate. Of the twenty senators who were up for reelection in 1978 and voted in favor of the treaties, only seven returned to serve again in January of 1979. (I hasten to note that both Senator Herman Talmadge and Senator Sam Nunn of Georgia supported the treaties.) Ambassadors Ellsworth Bunker and Sol Linowitz negotiated the original treaty terms for the United States, but at crucial times I had to deal directly from the White House with the leader of Panama, General Omar Torrijos. On almost a daily basis during the Senate debates, the Panamanian ambassador was with us to clarify issues, to resolve potential disputes with his government, or to work with individual senators.

SALT II negotiations, initiated by President Richard Nixon, were completed in my final talks with Soviet President Leonid Brezhnev in 1979 in Vienna. This time, there were three phases. The first involved me and other officials of our own government—the joint chiefs of staff and key advisers in the State Department and the Pentagon—in order to insure that our nation's position was understood and strongly supported among those who would later have to testify during ratification hearings. The second phase was with the Soviets, and required two and one-half years of work. Primarily because of the Soviet invasion of Afghanistan and opposition to the treaty from President Reagan, the third phase—ratification by the U. S. Senate—has not been completed. However, the treaty is still alive, and both sides are claiming to honor its basic terms.

Our U. N. Ambassadors Andrew Young and Donald McHenry did most of the preliminary negotiating to insure as peaceful a transition as possible from the Ian Smith regime of Rhodesia to the parliamentary elections which resulted in the democratically chosen Abel Muzorewa government of Zimbabwe. How to achieve majority rule in that African nation was a long-standing problem, and we played an important intermediate role, working closely with the British leaders who ultimately concluded the agreement establishing the new government.

MAJORITY RULE IN AFRICA

During my administration the most unpleasant and perhaps most dramatic negotiations in which we participated were with the various leaders of Iran after the seizure of American hostages in November 1979. The Algerians were finally chosen as the only intermediaries who were considered trustworthy both by me and the Ayatollah Khomeini. After many aborted efforts, final success was achieved during my last few hours in the White House. I was, of course, personally involved in each decision that was made during those final hours before the American prisoners were set free.

SECURING RELEASE OF HOSTAGES

Some of the most frustrating and at the same time the most gratifying negotiations were those

PEACE IN THE MIDDLE EAST

in which we sought to bring peace to the Middle
East—after four wars and thirty years of military
and political confrontation. We learned from
many sessions how to study issues, to bring negotiators together, to evolve general frameworks,
and then to reach detailed agreement.

RELATIONS
WITH
CHINA

The extremely sensitive interrelationships
among our country, China, and Taiwan had to be
considered as the United States moved toward
normalization with the most populous nation on
earth. Utmost secrecy was required until we
were ready to present publicly the final agreement, with its obvious advantages for our country. No progress was possible, however, until the
Chinese were convinced that we could be trusted
to face the adverse political reaction from the Taiwan Lobby in the United States—a problem that
had delayed the negotiating process since President Nixon had signed the Shanghai Commu-
nique in 1972.

EXTENT
OF U. S.
ROLE

In dealing with Brezhnev, Deng Xiaoping of
China, Torrijos, and Khomeini we were acting as
one of the two interested parties. With Ian
Smith, Muzorewa, Menachem Begin of Israel,
and Anwar Sadat of Egypt we were highly involved intermediaries.

POLITICAL
AGREEMENTS
IN
OVERVIEW

As I delineate some factors involved in these
varied negotiations, I want you to keep in mind
the complicated interrelationships among the U.
S. Congress, the American news media, public-
and special-interest groups, and leaders in Moscow, Panama, Iran, Jerusalem, Cairo, Peking,
and some of the capitals and jungles of Africa. In
each case we had to study the issues involved, un-

derstand the probable attitudes of all parties to the dispute, and determine whether negotiations were needed or advisable. Then we had to decide when to act, whether to make our first major efforts public or private, at what diplomatic level to initiate the contact, what forum to use, whether threats, warnings, or promises of reward would be advisable as part of our opening strategy, where likely opposition would arise in our own country to the negotiations themselves or to their prospective results and how to minimize this adverse effect, what nonrelated issues might create conflicts within our overall agenda, and at what point I should become personally and publicly involved. VARIABLES IN DISCUSSION

Realizing that when dealing with sovereign nations there is no judge or juror who can finally impose a settlement, we had to avoid the role of a litigant and devote a lot of time to assessing all sides of each question. It was especially important to understand the unique perspectives of those with whom we would be contending. We knew that a *voluntary* and *unanimous* decision would have to be reached. Often I would sit by a large globe, imagine myself to be Brezhnev, Sadat, Begin, Deng Xiaoping or Torrijos, and try to understand the issues in question from their points of view. At the same time, for me as president, the interests of the United States of America would always have to be paramount. VOLUNTARY, UNANIMOUS DECISIONS

In almost every case, the most difficult step was to obtain agreement as to when the negotiations should commence and who was to be included. Sometimes, particularly in a democracy, aroused public opinion can force action on reluc- WHEN TO BEGIN NEGOTIATION tant political leaders. All sides must be convinced there is a problem, that they can only resolve it together, and that the others are willing to bargain in good faith. In addition, the discussion process itself must be considered of potential benefit as a public forum and as a recognition of an issue's urgency. Those who desire to begin negotiations (including an interested third party) can sometimes take action—either in the form of reward or punishment—to create these necessary factors for the more reluctant parties.

HOW TO
MAINTAIN
DISCUSSION

There are many reasons why it is difficult to get talks started, and why there is a continuing problem in keeping them going. Repeatedly, we faced obstacles of this kind. Neither the Palestinians nor the Israelis would meet with the other; to do so would be the equivalent of official diplomatic recognition. Khomeini considered us devils incarnate, and issued unequivocal orders that *no* Iranian could negotiate with *any* American. Within a few weeks after Sadat's dramatic visit to Jerusalem broke an age-old stalemate, the two nations terminated all negotiations because of major incompatibilities in their "bottom line" demands. This impasse continued until the two leaders arrived at Camp David. Partially to retaliate against our strong human rights stand, the Soviets postponed further SALT negotiations for several months after Secretary of State Cyrus Vance in March of 1977 delivered to Moscow our proposal for deep mutual cuts in nuclear arsenals.

PATIENCE
AND
PERSISTENCE

Repeatedly, we learned that patience and persistence were required for ultimate success. Remember that the SALT II treaty was con-

cluded after more than six years of on-and-off negotiations under three presidents; the Law of the
Sea discussions continued for a decade; and the
Panama Canal treaty negotiations were concluded almost fourteen years after being initiated
by President Lyndon Johnson when violence
erupted in the Canal Zone just a few weeks after
he took office.

In each negotiating process it was desirable
to create an umbrella or general framework to
guide negotiators so that both sides would believe
it possible to reach their goals and not lose face—
to rationalize withdrawals from positions which
they had earlier taken in anger or during time of
war. This framework cannot be overly specific
and must permit maneuvering room, but at the
same time it cannot exclude the key issues in
contention.

For the Camp David talks, a general understanding was that, in exchange for peace and
more normal relations with Egypt, Israel would
substantially withdraw from the Sinai, and after
some interim period a final agreement would in-
clude Israeli withdrawal from territory in the
West Bank and Gaza and the granting of autonomy to the Palestinians who live there. With the
Iranians, the general formula was that the Algerians would help to negotiate the release of all the
American hostages in exchange for the return of
part of Iran's assets. For SALT II, our clearly de-
fined framework of discussions included limits
on launchers, missiles, and warheads which have
intercontinental range. Sometimes, when a broad
formula was impossible, we had to conclude one
or two relatively simple preliminary agreements

just to get some progress started—then build up step by step until a general formula began to take shape which could serve as a future guide.

One of the interesting features of international negotiations is the variation in technique and even basic attitudes exhibited by different nations. To Americans, a negotiation is most often looked upon as an obstacle to be overcome in order to reach a desired goal. We are inclined to be impatient and to accept or create deadlines to encourage more immediate action. We tend to make our concessions early and then cling tenaciously to proposals which we consider equitable. For the Soviets, on the other hand, it seemed to us that the same negotiation was almost an end in itself—a ritual that demonstrated to the world that they were equal in status to the United States and were sincerely trying to achieve an admirable goal. Their specific (and grudging) proposals were put forward quite late in the process and most often made in secret. They were obviously the result of a broad consensus within the Soviet bureaucracy. Obtaining quick decisions or responses from the Soviets was almost impossible. A surprising new proposal by us, even though ultimately acceptable to them, was looked upon with suspicion and disfavor.

ATTITUDES OF OTHER NATIONS

Substantive discussions on SALT had to be carried out at four distinct levels: through the professional negotiators of the tedious details at the daily talks in Geneva, with the Soviet ambassador in Washington for some tentative and exploratory proposals, between either Secretary Vance or me and Foreign Minister Andrei Gromyko for actual agreements, and ultimately at the

SOVIET OBSTINACY

summit with President Leonid Brezhnev for official ratification of what had already been decided. The seriousness of their proposals was
usually proportional to the seniority of the negotiator. Almost always proceeding from an original series of hard-line "nyets," progress was by
fits and starts, and seemed to work on what later
seemed to be a carefully orchestrated schedule. I
was always sure that the Soviets wanted a SALT
treaty, but it was like pulling teeth to get one
without sacrificing our own bargaining
positions.

The reliability of an opposing bargainer is
always a factor that must be considered. The Soviets are known to carry out the letter of an agreement, but to take advantage of every possible   OPPOSING
loophole they can find. The Chinese, on the   APPROACHES
other hand, will go out of their way to honor both
the letter and the spirit of what is decided. With
the Soviet Union you have to be sure to cross
every "t" and dot every "i" and eliminate all
doubt about what a particular phrase means. Of
course, when you negotiate on something as important as strategic arms limitations, the control
of nuclear weapons, caution is essential. Our policy was to exclude from the negotiations any subject or limits which could not be verified by our
own means. We never trusted the other side to assure that the terms of the agreement were being
carried out. I might add that ever since the first
SALT agreement was signed, many years ago,   HONORING
there has never been proof, as far as I know, that AGREEMENTS
either side has committed a major violation.
Complaints have usually been resolved almost
immediately and satisfactorily.

One of the most difficult problems that can intrude upon negotiations is the stream of uni-

lateral public statements which often flow from both sides to their own political constituencies. When these claims, demands, or promises preclude flexibility, they create new obstacles to progress. Had we not isolated the negotiators within the confines of Camp David and totally excluded the news reporters, I am convinced that we could never have reached agreement. Even then, Prime Minister Begin's provocative statements immediately after the accords were signed created nearly insurmountable obstacles to further progress toward a peace treaty.

Once the talks are under way, the negotiating parties must be constantly reminded of the

advantages of success versus the disadvantages of failure—always for both sides, never just for one. When a deadlock seems imminent, new approaches must be tried. If well prepared, each side will have many options ready to put forward—sometimes just a change in language—both to reach one's own goals and to react successfully to the proposals of others. Again, maximum understanding of one's adversary is crucial. Often it is possible to convince at least some key members of the opposing team and then let them use their influence to encourage movement toward agreement by the entire delegation. A real or implied threat that proposals will be made public sometimes helps to prevent the rejection of patently attractive or fair offers. We used this device in dealing with Prime Minister Begin, who was almost always the most recalcitrant member of the Israeli delegation. Sadat, by the way, was always the most constructive and generous among the Egyptians.

Although military, economic and political strength certainly favors the more powerful side, the matter of simple justice is a counterbalancing factor. Once the talks begin, there is at least some presumption that a final agreement will be fair to all affected people. However, this is not always helpful in convincing a party which has an advantage that negotiations should be commenced.

Concluding an agreement is often helped by some kind of deadline, either one set by the negotiators or one imposed from outside. The degree of known inevitability determines the effectiveness of this incentive to negotiate with dispatch. Without a deadline of some sort, talks tend to drag out almost interminably. The Mutual and Balanced Force Reductions talks between NATO and Warsaw Pact countries have continued for many years without detectable progress. It required more than 500 sessions to end the Korean War. Sometimes the leaders of nations even forget that the discussions are still ongoing. With the Panamanians in 1977, it was known that August 10 was the last day Ambassador Sol Linowitz could serve as negotiator. At Camp David we announced that we would leave on Sunday, 17 September 1978—either with or without an agreement. Khomeini and the Iranians knew that if our hostages were not released by noon on 20 January 1981, fresh negotiations would have to be commenced with the new Republican leaders in Washington. In all these cases substantial concessions were made at the last minute, and proved sufficient to reach agreements.

In closing, it may be interesting to apply some thoughts from these experiences to two of the most intractable and important issues now facing our government—nuclear arms talks and the Middle East peace process. You might remember these general rules which can help negotiations get started:

1. All parties must be convinced—by promise or threat—that the issues can and should be settled, and that they must be flexible. Public opinion is an important factor in convincing reluctant leaders to seek agreement.

2. Overt pressure to force others to negotiate is often counterproductive. Each must recognize that an unacceptable situation exists, that unilateral action cannot resolve it, and that one's overall circumstances will not improve without negotiation.

3. The agreement must ultimately be unanimous—so consider the basic needs of the adversaries. Fresh ideas are always necessary.

4. Repeated analyses of current circumstances will most often reveal opportunities for progress. Circumstances change, and insurmountable obstacles fade away. It should be assumed that both sides will have access to most of this information.

5. A proper forum is needed, and negotiators must be known to have authority to conclude agreements. The seriousness of intentions is indicated by the hierarchical status of the negotiator.

6. Negotiations with little prospect of complete success can sometimes be valuable in permitting the promulgation of views, the discovery of new alternatives, or the changing of previous positions with minimum embarrassment or loss of face.

7. It is best to start with a broad framework, compatible with existing agreements and encompassing enough issues to make some early successes possible.

In the Middle East dispute involving Israeli security (right now not much in doubt), occupied areas and Palestinian rights, several factors are preventing the initiation of serious negotiations. The most important is that the primary contenders—Israel, most Arabs and the Palestinians—will not talk to each other. Their public demands are totally incompatible: Prime Minister Begin's desire to take over the West Bank, Gaza and Golan Heights and to prevent self-determination among the people of the occupied territories vs. the refusal of the PLO and moderate Arabs to acknowledge the right of Israel to exist in peace behind defensible borders.

FACTORS AGAINST M. E. PEACE

Pressures continue to build. Israel's settlements policy is designed to create "facts" in the occupied territories, which later will be difficult to change. At the same time, the rapid taking of Palestinian family land is arousing intense opposition, and the result is growing violence and bloodshed. Many Jews and other friends of Israel see the continued deprivation of rights of the Palestinians as an unacceptable consequence of the military occupation, now in its sixteenth year. They also realize that even if the present Jewish

PALESTINIAN SOVEREIGNTY

population in the occupied areas is tripled or quadrupled, they will still constitute less than ten percent of the total. The absorption of another 1.3 million Arabs and Christians would change the character of Israel, and could give to non-Jews the balance of political power. Furthermore, failure to carry out the terms of the Camp David agreement in granting full autonomy to the Palestinians and withdrawing Israel's military government from the occupied territories is a danger to peace with Egypt.

SEARCH
FOR
LEADERSHIP

On the other side, there is now general realization among the Palestinian and Arab leaders that any armed conflict to change the status of Israel would be fruitless—at least for many years to come. The plight of his people is becoming more desperate, but Yassir Arafat, the PLO leader, is reluctant to anoint King Hussein of Jordan or anyone else to be spokesman for the four and one-half million Palestinians, and other moderate Arabs are not yet willing to force Arafat to change his position. Radical Arabs still insist that Israel can and must be destroyed militarily—if not now, then in the future. In the meantime, they are willing to let the Palestinians suffer.

U. S.
REINVOLVE-
MENT
REQUIRED

As in the past, those who want a settlement are looking to the United States to be a forceful mediator. However, for more than two years we have not been willing to assume this onerous duty. To resolve these difficult issues, the president of the United States and secretary of state must play a much stronger role. All sides depend on this, and there is no doubt that American security interests will be directly served by a settlement. Peace is impossible in the region if the extremists do not substantially modify their demands. The basic terms of the Camp David accords were incorporated in President Reagan's statement of September 1982, and can provide an overall framework (with mutually acceptable modifications) for an eventual settlement. This is one of the most complicated and imposing international disputes, but the importance of peace in the region warrants a maximum effort to resolve it. The first project of our new policy center in Atlanta, the Carter Center of Emory University, is to analyze this situation as completely as possible and to promulgate possible options or recommendations. The basic principles of dispute resolution cannot be ignored.

For the first time since Dwight Eisenhower was president, both American and Soviet negotiators do not seem to be bargaining in good faith to limit and reduce nuclear arsenals. Recent proposals from both sides are primarily designed for propaganda purposes, with the European public being the prime target. It is obvious that the demands cannot possibly be accepted by the other side, and that such unreasonable positions only subvert the prospects for agreement. Each side attacks the other in a growing stream of vituperation. We are accused by Mr. Andropov of being warmongers who believe that a limited nuclear war in Europe is acceptable and are devoting our primary national efforts to a massive and unwarranted buildup of U. S. armed forces in a fruitless desire for military superiority. President Reagan claims, on the other hand, that we are the epitome of goodness and righteousness—representing God himself in our dealings with the So-

BAD FAITH
IN
ARMS TALKS

viets, who are the personification of total evil. The official American assumption is that the Soviets have no desire for peace, cannot be trusted to negotiate in good faith or to carry out the terms of an agreement once made and are, in any case, doomed to early self-destruction because of the rot within their society.

BECOMING MORE FLEXIBLE

It is obvious why nuclear arms reduction talks have not been pursued at the top levels of authority, and the need to modify some of our attitudes is equally clear. Both we and the Soviets should reduce the public rhetoric, acknowledge the overriding need for serious negotiations to be conducted, have a modicum of mutual respect, admit that we are not the only ones who wish to avoid the escalating costs of expanding arsenals and the horrors of a nuclear war, and revert back to a situation where both sides are discussing the same subjects at a given time. Again, the task is not impossible if some basic principles of resolving disputes are applied.

CLOSING THOUGHTS

It would be naive to think that peace and justice can be achieved easily. No set of rules or study of history will automatically resolve the problems of overloaded courts or of extended, unnecessary litigation, or bring peace to Central America or the Middle East, or produce a nuclear arms agreement. However, with faith and perseverance, as exhibited during the long and fruitful lives of Carl Vinson and John Sibley, many equally complex problems in the past have been resolved in our search for justice and peace. They can be resolved in the future, provided, of course, that we can think of five new ways to measure the height of a tall building by using a barometer.

Scenes
from the
Inaugural Lecture

President Jimmy Carter tours the grounds of the Walter F. George School of Law in Macon, Georgia, in the company of (center) R. Kirby Godsey, president of Mercer University, and (left) Karl P. Warden, dean of the Law School.

Accompanied by agents of the United States Secret Service, President Carter and President Godsey (center) compare notes as they visit the campus of the Walter F. George School of Law with Dean Warden (left).

Prior to the dinner celebrating the Inaugural Lecture, President Carter shares a moment of relaxed good humor with with Robert L. Steed, author, Atlanta attorney, Law School alumnus, and chairman of the executive committee of the Mercer University Board of Trustees.

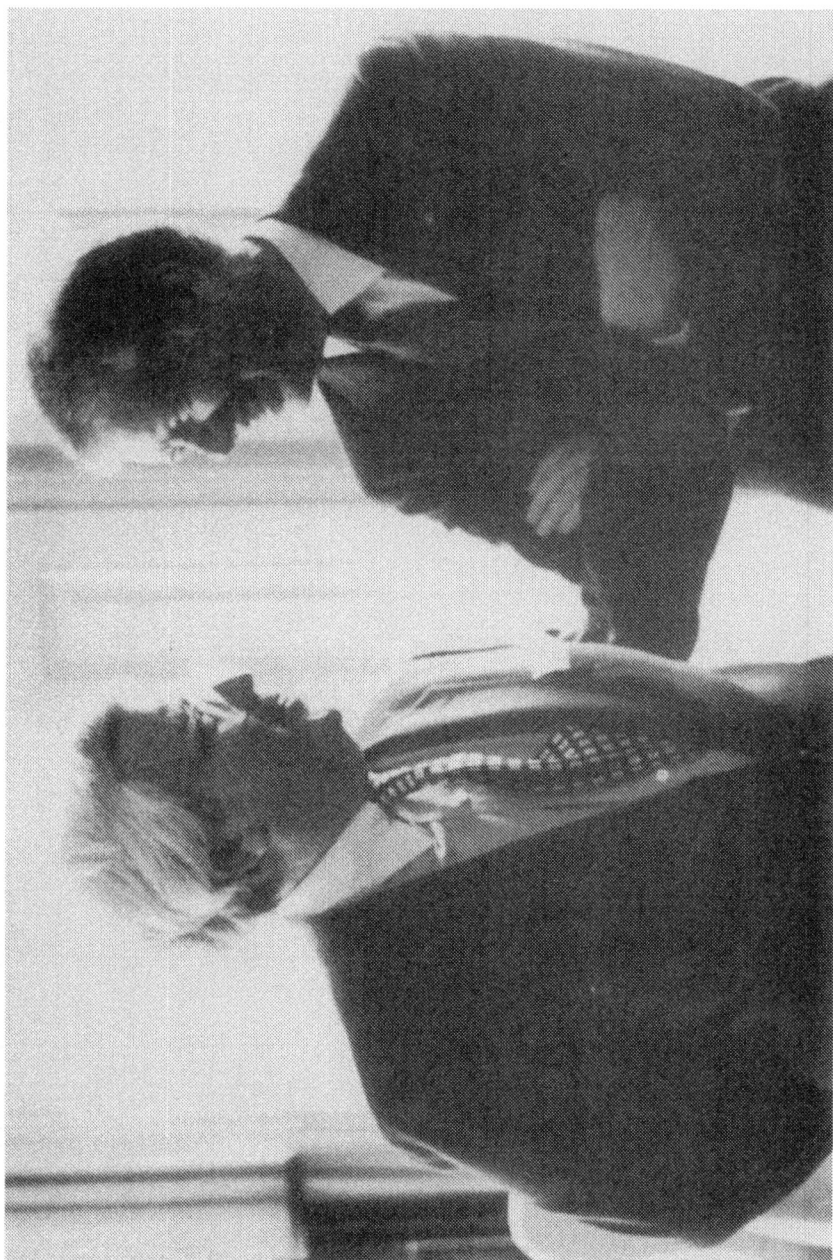

President Godsey welcomes President Carter to Mercer University and the Walter F. George School of Law during festivities at the Law School prior to the Inaugural Lecture.

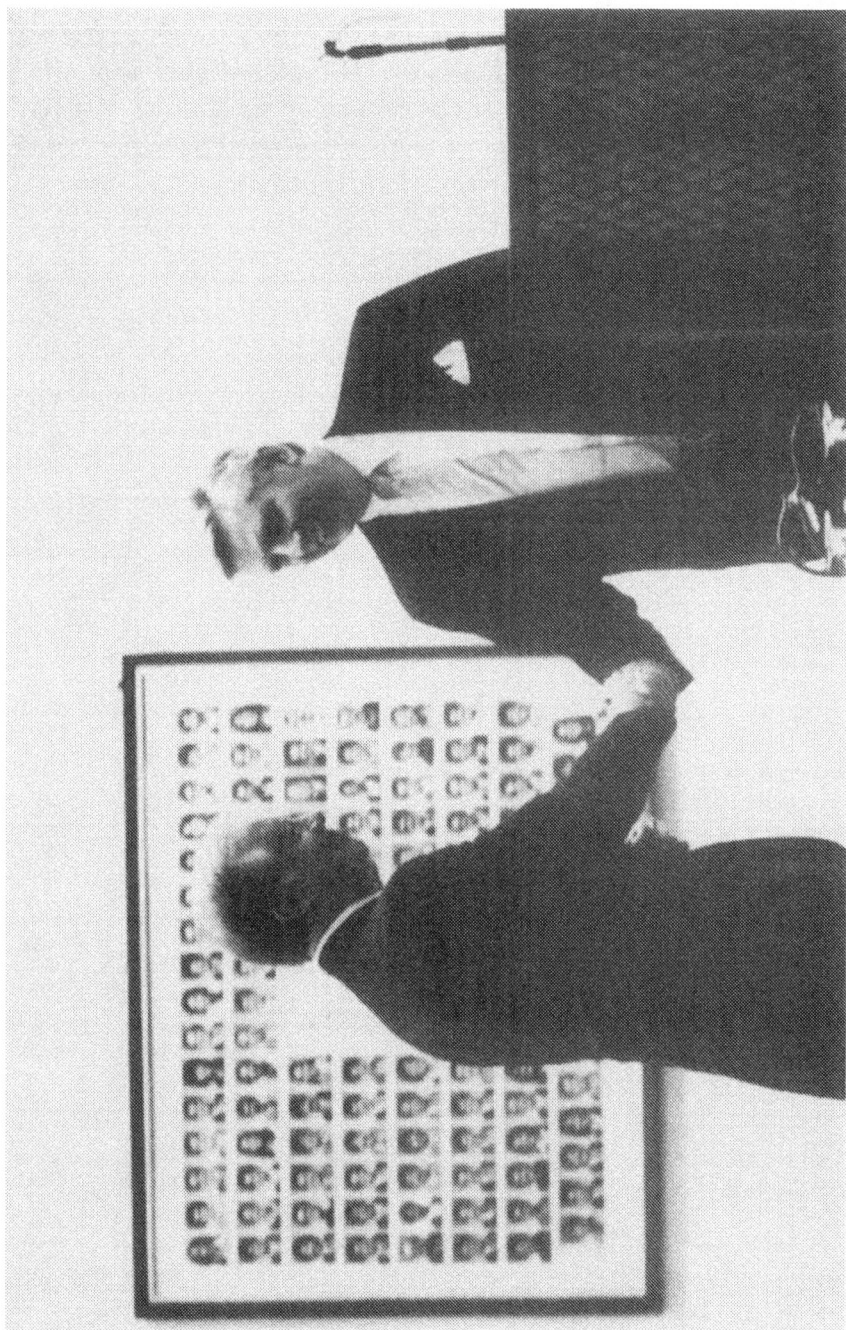

Following the dinner celebrating the Inaugural Lecture, President Carter poses with President Godsey and Dean Warden in the beautifully restored Woodruff House adjacent to the Walter F. George School of Law.

Just as the Inaugural Lecture of the Carl Vinson Memorial Lecture Series is about to begin, the speakers for the evening assemble on the stage of the Macon City Auditorium: (from left) Dean Karl P. Warden, Judge William A. Bootle, President R. Kirby Godsey, President Jimmy Carter, Robert L. Steed, and Lamar R. Plunkett, chairman of the Mercer University Board of Trustees.

As President Godsey welcomes the audience to the Inaugural Lecture and introduces the participants on the program, President Carter listens with Robert L. Steed and Lamar R. Plunkett of the Mercer University Board of Trustees.

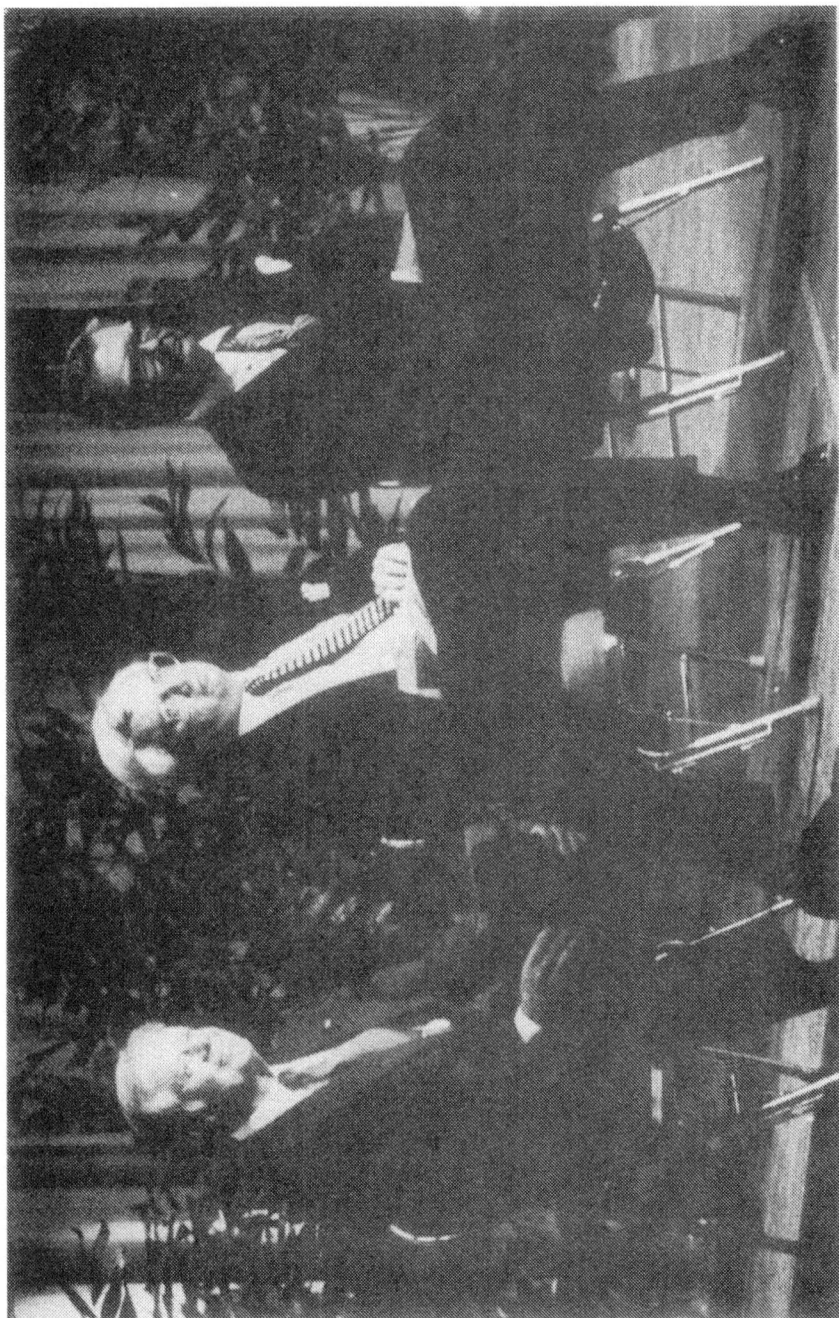

". . . a few highlights of an incredibly long and distinguished career as a lawyer, banker, farmer, and statesman": Robert L. Steed pays tribute to John Adams Sibley, a charter and life member of the Walter F. George Foundation, who "conceived, created, and personally endowed" the Carl Vinson Memorial Lecture Series.

President Carter and President Godsey listen as Robert L. Steed salutes John Adams Sibley, whose gift made possible the Carl Vinson Memorial Lecture Series.

"More than any other individual, Carl Vinson influenced and guided this nation through two world wars." Dean Karl P. Warden lauds one of the Law School's most distinguished alumni, whose service in the United States House of Representatives spanned half a century.

"We need . . . bright thinking, unanticipated approaches, and unorthodox ideas to achieve the ancient goals of better justice and peace in the world."

President R. Kirby Godsey listens with pleasure as President Carter delivers the Inaugural Carl Vinson Memorial Lecture.

"The legal profession must not look on reform with excessive timidity. Justice can be delivered more efficiently and fairly."

As President Carter delivers the Inaugural Lecture of the Carl Vinson Memorial Lecture Series, the other participants on the program join the audience in attentive appreciation: (from left) Dean Karl P. Warden, Judge William A. Bootle, President R. Kirby Godsey, Robert L. Steed, and Chairman Lamar R. Plunkett.

"Repeatedly, we learned that patience and persistence were required for ultimate success."

www.ingramcontent.com/pod-product-compliance
Lightning Source LLC
Chambersburg PA
CBHW020709270326
41928CB00005B/337